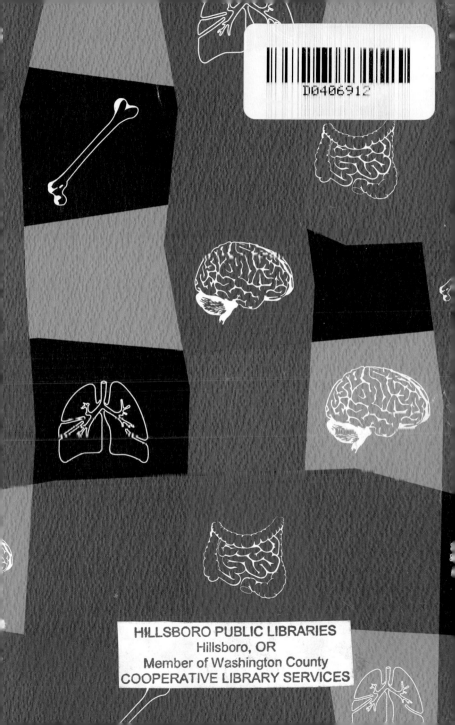

Special thanks to our adviser:
Susan Kesselring, M.A., Literacy Educator
Rosemount—Apple Valley—Eagan (Minnesota) School District

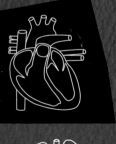

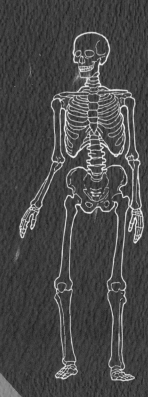

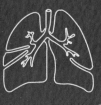

You Blink Twelve Times a Minute

and Other Freaky Facts
About the Human Body

by **Barbara Seuling**
illustrated by Ryan Haugen

PICTURE WINDOW BOOKS
Minneapolis, Minnesota

Editors: Christianne Jones and Emmeline Elliott
Designer: Abbey Fitzgerald
Page Production: Melissa Kes
Art Director: Nathan Gassman
The illustrations in this book were created digitally.

Picture Window Books
151 Good Counsel Drive
P.O. Box 669
Mankato, MN 56002-0669
877-845-8392
www.picturewindowbooks.com

All books published by Picture Window Books
are manufactured with paper containing at least
10 percent post-consumer waste.

Library of Congress Cataloging-in-Publication Data
Seuling, Barbara.
You blink twelve times a minute and other freaky facts about the
human body / by Barbara Seuling ; illustrated by Ryan Haugen.
p. cm. — (Freaky facts)
Includes index.
ISBN-13: 978-1-4048-4116-1 (library binding)
ISBN-13: 978-1-4048-4121-5 (paperback)
1. Body, Human—Miscellanea—Juvenile literature. 2. Medicine—
Miscellanea—Juvenile literature. I. Haugen, Ryan, 1972- II. Title.
QP37.S4895 2009
612—dc22

4099 7958 03/09

2008006340

Table of Contents

Chapter 1

A Good Head on Your Shoulders:
Your Brain and Facial Features

People blink their eyes an average of 12 times per minute.

The human brain weighs about 3 pounds (1.35 kg). If all of the water was squeezed out, the brain would weigh less than a can of soda.

It takes less than 1 second for the message of pain in your big toe to reach your brain.

Brain cells are the only cells in the body that are not replaced. The supply you have now must last the rest of your life.

Your brain uses the same amount of power that would light a 10-watt lightbulb.

After the brain, the eye is the most complex organ in the body.

Only one out of three people in the world has perfect vision, which is 20/20.

On the inside corner of your eye is the remnant of a third eyelid. Some animals still have this protective lid after their birth.

Eyes will take in about 24 million images in an average lifetime.

The fastest muscles in your body are the ones that help your eyes blink.

Why do you get dizzy when you spin around? Because there is liquid in your inner ear that spins around with you. When you stop, the liquid keeps moving. That's what gives you a dizzy feeling.

Some of the earliest hearing aids were shaped like trumpets and held to the ear.

A Pakistan man, Zafar Gill, lifted a 113-pound, 15-ounce (51.7-kg) weight with his ear in 2004.

A man from India has ear hair that is 5.19 inches (13.2 cm) long.

Each of the tiny bumps on your tongue contains about 50 to 150 taste buds. Each taste bud is sensitive to only one flavor type—sweet, salty, sour, or bitter.

Most of your taste buds are on your tongue. About 10 percent are on the upper part of your mouth and inside of your cheeks.

You cannot taste food unless it is mixed with saliva.

The only letter sounds you can make without your tongue are m, p, h, f, and v.

Your tongue is the most movable organ in your body. It can move in every direction. It has plenty of muscle and no bone.

The world's longest tongue belonged to an Italian man. It measured 3.74 inches (9.5 cm).

In 2004, a British man emitted the world's loudest burp.

An ordinary nose can distinguish from 10,000 to 40,000 different smells.

According to some experts, noses adapt to do a particular job in their native regions. In hot, dry places like Egypt, people have long noses that moisturize the air as it is inhaled. In humid climates like Kenya, where there is no need for extra moisture, people have short, flat noses. In cold places like Finland, people have long narrow noses that warm the air as it is inhaled.

A Chinese woman has grown her hair since 1973, when she was 13 years old. In 2004, her hair measured 18-feet, 5.5-inches (5.7-m) long.

A 12-year-old California boy balanced 15 stainless steel spoons on his face in 2004.

The small town of Egremont, England, has hosted the World Gurning Championships since 1267. During this competition, participants put their head through a horse collar and try to make the ugliest face.

In 1999, Englishman John Evans balanced a 352-pound (158.4-kg) car on his head for 33 seconds.

Beginnings and Endings:
Life and Death

The king of Siam (now called Thailand) fathered 370 children by the time he died in 1910.

Every human being spent about half an hour as a single cell.

The Pygmy women of Africa are the smallest full-grown females on Earth. However, they have the largest babies in the human race. The newborns average more than 8 pounds (3.6 kg) at birth.

On February 9, 2003, the largest newborn on record was born in Italy. Tomasso Cipriani weighed 28 pounds (12.6 kg), 4 ounces (112 g).

In 2004, the world's smallest surviving baby was born in Chicago. Rumaisa Rahman weighed 8.6 ounces (240.8 g), which is less than a can of soda. She measured less than 10 inches (25.4 cm) long.

A woman in Russia had 69 children. She gave birth to 16 pairs of twins, seven sets of triplets, and four sets of quadruplets.

Quadruplets occur once in every 650,000 births. Identical quadruplets occur once in 64 million births.

One out of every 90 births in the United States results in twins.

A Romanian woman gave birth to a boy on December 11, 2004. Fifty-nine days later, she delivered his twin brother.

In 1800, American women had an average of seven children. Today, American women have an average of two children.

In the United States, more babies are born in the months of August and September than any other time of the year.

An English girl born in 2007 was given 25 middle names. Each name is a tribute to a famous boxer: Autumn Sullivan Corbett Fitzsimmons Jeffries Hart Burns Johnson Willard Dempsey Tunney Schmeling Sharkey Carnera Baer Braddock Louis Charles Walcott Marciano Patterson Johansson Liston Clay Frazier Foreman Brown.

Albert Einstein was born with a large, misshapen head. His mother initially thought her son's head was deformed. Einstein's head eventually became a normal shape, and he became a scientific genius.

Human life expectancy has doubled in the last 200 years.

The average life span of a caveman was about 18 years. In the United States today, the average life span is about 74 years for men and 79 years for women.

Some scientists believe that humans have the potential to live around 150 years.

In 1635, a 152-year-old man named Thomas Parr was discovered living in the English countryside. He was brought to London and presented to the king. He was given employment in a noble household and supplied with plenty of food and drink. In a short time, he died of an overly rich diet.

LORDY, LORDY
LOOK WHO'S 152!
HAPPY BIRTHDAY!

In ancient Greece, children were legally responsible to care for elderly parents. The children also had to provide their parents with an appropriate send off after death.

Body snatching was a common practice in 19th-century Scotland. Medical students were always in need of new bodies to dissect and study the anatomy. The most likely place to get the bodies was from newly-dug graves. Relatives often guarded the graves of loved ones until the body was too decomposed to dissect.

Nails and hair look as if they continue growing after a person has died, but they don't. They appear longer because the skin around the hair and nails dries and shrinks.

A rare modern-day mummy is the body of Vladimir Lenin. He was a political leader of the Soviet Union. His body has been preserved and put on display for the public since his death in 1924. The government will not give away the secret of how the body was preserved.

The man who popularized jogging in America, James Fixx, died of a heart attack while running.

In 1396, 6-year-old Princess Isabelle of France was married to 29-year-old King Richard II of England. She was a widow by the time she was 10.

When the inventor of the modern Frisbee, Ed Headrick, died, his ashes were molded into Frisbees.

A Hitch in the System:
Strange Ailments, Hiccups, and Snoring

Girls of well-to-do families in 18th-century
Europe often had greenish complexions.
Experts say it was the result of not eating
enough, wearing corsets that were too tight,
and not exercising.

Louis Pasteur, the famed scientist, carried a
portable microscope with him. He used it to
see if the food served at friends' homes was
safe to eat.

Hippocrates (460–377 B.C.), the father of medicine, was the first to describe the flu.

In the 18th century, a noblewoman died from regularly painting her face with white lead.

Queen Elizabeth I stuffed her mouth with cloth when she appeared in public because her face had sunk in from the loss of her front teeth.

Queen Victoria of England, later learned to be a carrier of the blood disease hemophilia, spread the disease through just about every royal house in Europe. Her children, inheritors of the disease, married into other royal families.

Alexander I of Greece died from blood poisoning after he was bitten by a pet monkey.

In the Middle Ages, it was believed that leprosy could be spread through the breath as well as through physical contact. Lepers were required by law to stand downwind if they stopped to speak to anyone on a road.

Stone Age human fossils show evidence that our early ancestors suffered some of the same complaints of the body as people today.

About two-thirds of the estimated 620,000 casualties of the Civil War (1861–1865) were due to disease, not from injuries that occurred while fighting in the war.

Eating one death cap, the world's deadliest mushroom, is fatal. Immediate medical attention should be sought, or death will occur within one to two weeks.

Tapeworms can grow to 32 feet (9.8 m) long inside the human intestine.

In 1848, Phineas P. Gage was preparing to blast a large rock at a construction site, when an explosion sent an iron rod through his skull. The rod was removed, with no apparent harm done to the man. However, people who knew him said afterward his gentle manner was gone. He was prone to outbursts of bad temper.

Laughing sickness, or *kuru*, is a rare disease that affects only the Fore tribe of New Guinea. No one survives it.

An average case of the hiccups lasts for five minutes.

Men hiccup more than women.

The hiccups of a young man admitted to an English hospital in 1769 were heard one-half mile (0.8 km) away.

An Iowa man named Charles Osborne hiccupped 20 to 40 times per minute every day from 1922 to 1990. That's 69 years with the hiccups! He said the hiccups started when he tried to lift a 350-pound (157.5-kg) hog.

It is estimated that 37 million Americans snore while they sleep. Some experts believe that snoring is linked back to the cavemen, who made terrifying noises in their sleep to frighten away savage beasts.

The highest recorded decibel level for a human snore is 92, about the sound of heavy traffic at an intersection.

A few rare human beings are born with a visible tail. Everyone has a tailbone, but usually it is hidden beneath the surface of the skin.

Healings and Dealings:
Medications, Surgeries, and Other Remedies

Honey was the most commonly used medicine among ancient Egyptians.

At one time, people used horseradish to treat baldness. Ancient Egyptians used hippo fat to prevent baldness.

There is proof that Stone Age people performed surgical operations. They would saw off limbs with tools made of stone.

In ancient Babylon, sick people were laid in the public square. Everyone passing by had to ask about the person's ailment and offer a remedy if possible.

The Aztecs began eating arsenic regularly as children to build up their immunity to the poison.

In Colonial days, one of the cures for a toothache was to rub brimstone and gunpowder mixed with butter onto the gums.

The Turks of ancient Anatolia fed cooked bird tongues to children who were slow in learning to talk.

Egyptians used moldy bread to treat infected wounds, and it worked. Some say it was a forerunner of penicillin, which was developed from mold. Today, penicillin is used to fight off infections.

Thrush, an infection of the mouth, was once treated by putting a live frog in the patient's mouth.

Chapter Four

In the 18th and 19th centuries, leeches were used to treat the sick. Several leeches were applied to the affected part of a sick person's body. For example, to cure a headache, leeches were applied in a ring around the head.

No longer a cure belonging to past centuries, doctors and veterinarians all over the world use maggots and leeches to treat wounds today.

The ancient Chinese paid their doctors for keeping them well. They stopped paying them if they became sick.

Powdered mummy was once an important ingredient in European medicine. When the supply of mummies dwindled, "new" mummies were made from recent corpses.

One type of alternative medicine uses the powder of crushed jewels to rejuvenate the body.

One surgeon's favorite hobby, sailing, helped him cure one of his patients, who had a severe curve in her spine. The doctor implanted a device modeled after the one that helped keep the sails tight on his boat. This gadget held the patient's muscles tight so that the spine straightened.

One folk remedy for hiccups is to cover your head with a wastebasket and have somebody beat on it. Another is to drink nine swallows of water from your grandfather's cup without taking a breath. Still another is to spit on a rock, then turn it over. Or you can wet a piece of red thread with your tongue, stick it to your forehead, and look at it.

Many cultures in history have used human and animal urine for healing. Hindu yogic communities drank their urine to promote general health. Saharan Arabs used their urine to clean the wounds of British soldiers in World War II (1939–1945).

Morarji Desai, prime minister of India from 1977 to 1979, lived to be 99 years old. Desai attributed his good health to drinking his own urine every day.

Before anesthesia was discovered, a surgeon established his reputation by the speed with which he could operate. Famous surgeon Robert Liston is said to have cut off his assistant's fingers in his hurry to get the job done.

When 64-year-old Polish countess Rosa Branicka was told that she had breast cancer, she took the matter into her own hands. Refusing her doctors' help, the countess traveled Europe, gathering medical instruments. She then went to a hotel room in Paris and operated on herself. Branicka successfully removed the tumor and lived to be 82.

Dogs in the United States and Britain are being trained to sniff out certain types of cancer.

Sofie Herzog, a pioneer doctor in Texas, removed so many bullets from gunfighters that she made a necklace of them. She wore it throughout her life. The necklace was buried with her.

Cardinal Richelieu, French prime minister in 1624, jumped over furniture every day as exercise.

Back in the Day:
Beliefs, Customs, and Medical Marvels

Francesco A. Lentini, known as the Three-Legged Wonder, was born with three fully-developed legs. He could walk, run, jump, ride a bicycle, ride a horse, ice skate, drive his own car, and kick a soccer ball with each of his legs. Lentini boasted that he was the only man who came equipped with his own chair, using the third and shortest leg as a stool.

In 1770, British Parliament declared a marriage would be null and void if a woman had used artificial devices to make a man marry her. Artificial teeth, wigs, and high-heeled shoes were considered fraudulent.

On the Sandwich Islands, chiefs were once accompanied by servants carrying portable spittoons. It was believed that if they could capture some of their enemy's saliva, they would be able to bewitch him.

Bronze Age people used drugs to fight illness but not by repairing the body. Drugs were used mainly to chase away the evil spirits that inhabited the body, causing the ailment.

People once believed that the mucus that comes out of your nose when you have a cold was from your brain leaking.

Peter Stuyvesant, governor of Colonial New York, lost his leg during a battle on a Caribbean island in 1644. The leg was amputated, given a Christian burial, and given full military honors. Meanwhile, the rest of Stuyvesant went on to live another 28 years.

In 1793, a girl with one eye in the middle of her forehead was born in France. She lived to be 15.

Conjoined twins Chang and Eng Bunker were born joined at the chest in 1811. They grew up, married a pair of American sisters, fathered a total of 21 children, and died within three hours of each other in 1874. The brothers, who were originally from Siam (now called Thailand), became so famous that the term "Siamese twins" was coined. It is still sometimes used to describe conjoined twins.

The British once believed that it would take a freckle-faced king to conquer the Welsh.

The Maya people thought it was attractive to sharpen their teeth to points and to have crossed eyes.

Ancient Chinese used to grow their fingernails very long to show their high status. Long nails showed that they didn't have to work. Women wore finger guards made of gold, silver, and jade to protect their nails.

Queen Elizabeth I took a bath once a month. Queen Isabella of Spain bathed only twice in her life—when she was born and when she was married.

Seeking "ancient greatness," King Charles II was known to rub powder from mummified Egyptian kings on himself.

Women in Italy used to put drops of juice from the poisonous belladonna plant in their eyes to enlarge their pupils. They believed this would make them appear more beautiful.

French queen Isabeau of Bavaria tried to maintain her beauty by putting a mixture of boar brains, crocodile glands, and wolf blood on her face.

In 18th-century Scotland, citizens sometimes gathered at an execution. They would collect the criminal's blood, which was believed to cure various diseases.

Frederick the Great of Prussia hated water and almost never washed his hands or face. Instead, he painted his cheeks each morning with red paint to look fresh and healthy.

Soap, which dates back to ancient Babylon, was not used by Europeans for cleaning the body until the 17th century.

It is believed in some primitive cultures that a person's spirit enters and leaves the body through the mouth. Therefore, a well-meaning friend might try to keep the spirit from leaving by holding the person's mouth and nose closed.

Frederic Chopin, the famous composer, was so afraid of being buried alive that he asked his friends to cut open his body before they buried him. His friends obliged, and Chopin's heart was sent to his native Poland.

In the 1800s, people had the bumps on their heads read. The idea was that bumps indicated a particularly strong area of the brain, indicating the person's special abilities.

A person in Japan is more likely to ask your blood type than your astrological sign. The Japanese believe people with certain blood types have particular personality traits. Some employers even show preference to certain employees because of their blood types.

A Hindu fakir of Bengal, India, extended his right arm above his head in 1902 and kept it that way for 10 years. He did it to show he could conquer pain. He never took his arm down, even when a bird built its nest in the fakir's open palm. When he died, he was buried with his arm extended.

People once thought that a sneeze was a sign that death was near. That's why people say "God bless you."

Some people believe that the cow's tongue stimulates the naked scalp, helping to make hair grow. A farmer near Trier, Germany, sells licks from his cow to help bald people.

On the American frontier, there was a folk remedy for every complaint. To rid oneself of birthmarks, it was necessary to rub them with the hand of a corpse or the head of a live eel three mornings in a row. A frontiersman in the northern forests would fasten the right eye of a wolf inside his right sleeve to ward off illness.

Western frontier miners of the 19th century believed that if they followed the knocking sound made by ghosts of miners who had died there, called Tommyknockers, they would be led to gold.

In medieval times, if a man's eyebrows touched each other, he was believed to be a werewolf.

It was once believed that a vein ran from the third finger of the left hand to the heart. The wedding ring came to be worn on that finger as a symbol of love.

The early Greeks told stories to explain the world. One was of a woman named Pandora. She owned a box holding all evils and disease. Although she had been warned not to, she opened the box and all of the contents escaped, and sickness came into the world.

Glossary

ailments—illnesses

amputated—cut off

ancestors—relatives who lived several generations ago

anesthesia—the loss of all feeling

arsenic—a kind of poison

casualties—people injured or killed in an accident or a war

cells—small, basic units of living matter

complexions—the color of people's skin

conjoined—joined together

decomposed—broken down

disease—a condition that prevents the body from functioning properly

dissect—to cut up and study

execution—to kill according to a legal order

fossils—the remains of a plant or animal that lived between thousands and millions of years ago

intestine—a long tube in the body that carries and digests food and stores waste products; it is divided into the small and the large intestine

leprosy—a disease that attacks the nerves, skin, and muscles

muscle—a tissue in the body that is made of strong fibers; muscles can be tightened or relaxed to make the body move

organ—a body part that is made up of tissue and does a particular job

preserved—kept from being lost, damaged, or decayed

quadruplets—four children born at the same time to the same mother

saliva—the clear liquid that keeps the mouth moist

spine—the backbone

vein—one of the blood vessels that carry blood to the heart

widow—a woman whose husband is dead and who has not married again

Index

To Learn More

More Books to Read

Berger, Melvin, and Gilda Berger. *You're Tall in the Morning but Shorter at Night: and Other Amazing Facts About the Human Body.* New York: Scholastic, 2004.

Brewer, Sarah. *1,001 Facts About the Human Body.* New York: DK, 2002.

Rosenberg, Pam. *Eew! Icky, Sticky, Gross Stuff in Your Body.* Mankato, Minn.: Child's World, 2008.

On the Web

FactHound offers a safe, fun way to find Web sites related to topics in this book. All of the sites on FactHound have been researched by our staff.

1. Visit *www.facthound.com*
2. Type in this special code: 1404841164
3. Click on the FETCH IT button.

Your trusty FactHound will fetch the best sites for you!

Look for all of the books in the Freaky Facts series:

- Ancient Coins Were Shaped Like Hams and Other Freaky Facts About Coins, Bills, and Counterfeiting
- Cows Sweat Through Their Noses and Other Freaky Facts About Animal Habits, Characteristics, and Homes
- Earth Is Like a Giant Magnet and Other Freaky Facts About Planets, Oceans, and Volcanoes
- It Never Rains in Antarctica and Other Freaky Facts About Climate, Land, and Nature
- One President was Born on Independence Day and Other Freaky Facts About the 26th through 43rd Presidents
- Some Porcupines Wrestle and Other Freaky Facts About Animal Antics and Families
- There are Millions of Millionaires and Other Freaky Facts About Earning, Saving, and Spending
- Three Presidents Died on the Fourth of July and Other Freaky Facts About the First 25 Presidents
- You Blink Twelve Times a Minute and Other Freaky Facts About the Human Body
- Your Skin Weighs More Than Your Brain and Other Freaky Facts About Your Skin, Skeleton, and Other Body Parts

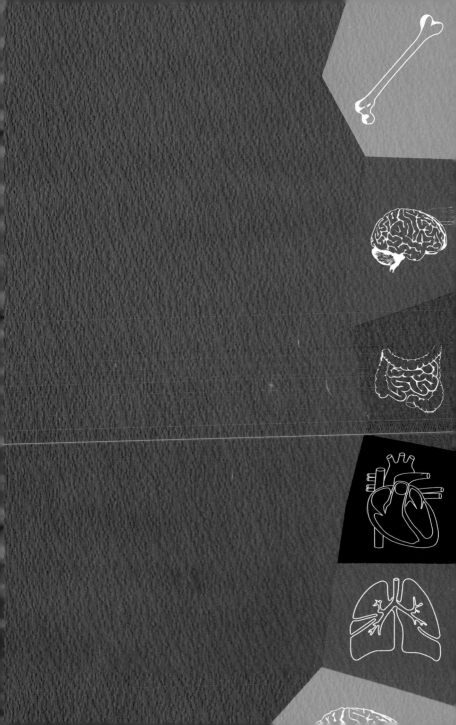

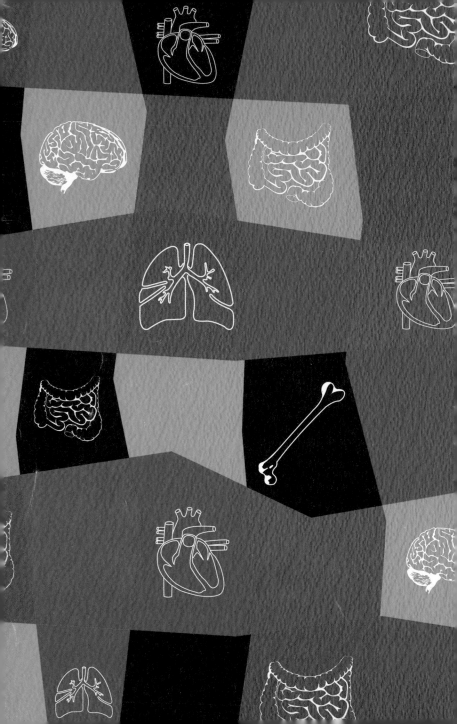